My Palestinian Village

Written & Illustrated by
Luqman Nagy

Helping you build a family of faith

This book is dedicated to
Shaikh 'Abd al-Hamid Bin Booh, my dear
Palestinian friend and travelling companion during
my visit to Jerusalem, the eternal capital of Palestine.

Goodword Books Pvt. Ltd.
1, Nizamuddin West Market
New Delhi-110 013
E-mail: info@goodwordbooks.com
Printed in India
First published 2004
© Goodword Books 2004

www.goodwordbooks.com

INTRODUCTION

For the past half century, media coverage of the Palestinian problem has been relentless. During this time, the world has witnessed the noble people of Palestine being denied their rights by a brutal occupying force.

What often goes unreported, however, is the day-to-day inhumanity of occupation. For centuries, the Palestinian village was a thriving entity–self-contained and self-sustaining. Today, with ancient olive groves–the life-blood of the rural economy – being uprooted and roadblocks preventing agricultural produce from reaching its market, the Palestinian village is under threat of extinction.

The Palestinians of today are the true *ibna' filastin*, "the sons of Palestine"–the rightful owners of the land that they have tilled, farmed and nurtured for thousands of years. The Palestinian "diaspora" (the forced flight of refugees out of their homeland) is a recent phenomenon: the direct result of the establishment of the state of Israel in 1948.

This book introduces the young Muslim reader to the village life of a Palestinian boy in today's world. 'Abd al-Salaam not only knows his history well, but speaks to us with a sincere Islamic conviction. In no part of Palestine can one escape the injustice of the illegal occupation. Still, most Palestinians have shown great patience and have heeded Allah who has said in the Qur'an: "Endure, then, with patience–always remembering that it is none but Allah who gives you the strength to endure adversity." (*surah al-nahl: ayah 127*)

To you all my salaams.

Luqman Nagy
Ramadhan 2003

King Fahd University,
Dhahran, Saudi Arabia

1. My Lovely Village

My name is 'Abd al-Salaam and I am a thirteen year old Palestinian boy. I am a Muslim, *al-Hamdulillah* and live in a very ancient part of the world. "Welcome to my beloved country of Palestine", or, as we say in Arabic: *ahlan bikum fi baladi al-'aziz filastin*. A sign in three languages (Arabic, English and Hebrew) also welcomes you to our village.

We learn in our history books that Palestine (*filastin*) was the birth- place of agriculture. In fact, the very first communities of settled farmers lived right here in the region around Jericho. That was almost 9,000 years ago!

Today, the climate is much harsher than it was all those years ago. Still, underground sweet water reservoirs and water diverted from the River Jordan help us irrigate our small gardens. My village is called Bayt Zaytun because for hundreds of years my Palestinian ancestors have grown olives on the sloping hills in the area. My father tends our olive trees just as his father and grandfather had done before him.

My house is on the edge of the olive grove, just behind our mosque. Can you see the Palestinian flag my brother and I made that is proudly flying from our rooftop? For years, it was forbidden to fly our flag and many people were imprisoned for carrying it. Each morning, I go to the village mosque and read the Holy Qur'an before prayers. Arabic is my language and *alHamdulillah*, reading *kitab Allah* fills me with strength. It helps me understand what is really true (*haqq*) and what is false (*batil*) in this world.

When I return home from the mosque, I see my flag fluttering in the crisp morning air and sometimes I begin to sing our national anthem: *baladi, baladi, baladi, ardhi, ya ardh al-judud*. "My country, my country, my country, my land, land of my grandfathers."

I am a young Muslim boy, but even I know that history neither lies nor forgives. In Palestine, we have many meaningful proverbs, one of which is the following: "He who doesn't ask questions of the elderly is guideless." I have spoken to the knowledgeable elders in our village and have listened to their wise words ever since I was a small child. I now know the true history of my country, *al-Hamdulillah*.

2. My Village House

Here is my beautiful village home in Bayt Zaytun. It is one of the oldest houses in our village and is made of blocks of honey yellow limestone. Such stone is hard to come by in our part of Palestine, so for centuries most villagers have used the traditional building material—mud and straw—to construct their homes, mosques and schools.

Bayt Zaytun is not far from the Dead Sea which is 400 metres below sea level. It is, therefore, not only the lowest point on Earth but is also the world's saltiest body of water. For our crops, we depend mainly on cisterns that collect the infrequent rain water to irrigate our crops and to supply water to our livestock. Occasionally in winter, it will get very cold and for a day or two we might even see snow! Fresh drinking water is always a problem in our part of the world. *Al-Hamdulillah*, in our village there are several old wells from which we can still take water from deep underground. But the number of wells are fewer than in the past. We live under occupation and since 1967 have not been permitted to dig any new ones. We, therefore, value every drop of fresh water and of course waste none.

A fig tree and a variety of herbs grow near the well in front of our house. Fresh *na'nah* (mint), *baqdoonus*

(parsley) and *kuzbarah* (coriander) are all used in Palestinian cooking. Palestine is the land of the fig and olive. Allah has selected these two trees in particular as symbols and has mentioned them in *surah al-tin*. Both are very special trees which provide us with not only a succulent fruit, but also a nutritious food that yields the most healthful of all cooking oils, *masha'Allah*.

We are fortunate here in Bayt Zaytun. *Al-Hamdulillah*, with the careful use of water, our villagers are able to grow lemons, melons, grapes and even bananas on very tiny plots of land. Other villages have suffered more from the occupation and have even had their mature olive and fruit trees uprooted! This must be considered yet one more inexcusable crime, surely punishable on *yawm al-hesab* (the Day of Judgement).

3. Our Palestinian Food

We Palestinians are people of the earth. This beloved homeland we call *filastin* is one of the few really sacred places on Earth. It is the land of Prophets, many of whom are mentioned in the Qur'an. My father, uncles and cousins all till this ancient land. However, our farms and gardens can not compare in size with those of neighbouring countries. Still, each year we sow our crops and give thanks to Allah for all His bounty. Just as an attentive shepherd knows each and every sheep in his flock, our villagers are equally familiar with every single olive tree in their groves. Only a farmer or a shepherd can fully understand how attached we are to the earth; our roots lie deep.

Today, we have guests for lunch and my mother has prepared some delicious Palestinian dishes. *Insha'Allah*, we will sit in our *majlis*, or sitting room and eat off a *sini* (a large round tray) covered with an old *kaffiyah* (Palestinian head-covering) which we use as a table cloth. In the centre of the table is a very famous Palestinian favourite: *maqlubah* or "upside down" rice and eggplant casserole. The tomato, cucumber, mint, onion and lettuce salad with small squares of toasted flat bread is the very tasty *fattoush*. All the ingredients come from our small vegetable garden, *al-Hamdulillah*. My aunt came this morning and baked the round flat bread you see here. She covered the dough before baking

9

with a blend of dried thyme, sumaq, sesame seeds and spices mixed with our own olive oil. This "herb bread" called *zaatar* is incredibly delicious; we believe it makes one strong and helps clear the mind! I always eat *zaatar* before I enter any major exams at school. The wonderful fresh buttermilk drink called *laban* is made from the milk of our neighbour's cow.

Hanging on our wall you can see a photograph of *al-qubbah al-sakhra* (the Dome of the Rock), an important symbol for all Muslims, and a reminder, especially to us, that *al-quds* (Jerusalem) is the eternal capital of Palestine. Next to this picture is a large key. This is yet another symbol. It belongs to my grandfather's brother (great uncle) who was forced to leave his house in the western part of Palestine when his land was occupied in 1948.

For as long as I can remember, I have seen this key, hanging unmoved on our wall. As a child, I used to ask my father about it: "Ya, Baba! Will this key ever be used again to open a door?" I am still asking this question today!

4. The Amazing Olive Tree

The olive tree is truly amazing! It thrives even in the rocky, dry areas of Palestine; it is indeed the lifeblood of Palestinian agriculture. For the villagers of Bayt Zaytun, the olive tree is a blessing. When the olive harvest begins—usually at the end of September each year—our village comes to life as everyone becomes involved in the work.

We hear about modern machines that are used in some countries to pick olives. These are very costly so we rely on the traditional method of harvesting using buckets and ladders. We typically use sticks and rakes to knock the olives off the trees onto a canvas matting or blanket. To make the picking easier, we have always planted our olive trees close together. My father believes

that the old-fashioned harvesting techniques maximize the quality of the fruit.

Each day, we get up early and, after praying *salat al-fajr* and eating a hearty breakfast, head off to work in the olive groves. It usually takes about five years for an olive tree to produce any fruit, but after this, they

This beautiful silver dirham from the time of the first 'Ayyubid ruler, Salah al-Din, the liberator of al-quds (Jerusalem), was in use all over Palestine. On this coin, the kalimah has been placed in the margin. The beautiful Kufic script in the square reads al-malik a-nasir salah al-dunya wa ad-din ("the defending king [Salah al-Din], Honour of the World and the Faith"). Coins like these are requently unearthed in the fields around Bayt Zaytun reminding us of the glorious Islamic history of Palestine.

can often live for hundreds of years and still bear fruit. My father believes that some of the world's oldest olive trees grow in Palestine.

When an older tree dies, it is a sad occasion, but new trees can be easily planted from the branches of living ones.

Olives change colour as they ripen. From pale green, they change to yellow, red, dark purple and finally black. After harvesting the olives, we place them in 40-50 kilo bags. Raw olives are too bitter to be eaten and must first be soaked in a solution of salt, lemon juice and some- times a spice mixture. The olives we harvest for olive oil must be black before being sent to large olive presses located in towns like Ramallah. Unfortunately, due to the occupation of our land, road-blocks and closures sometimes prevent us from transporting our olives to market.

For as long as we have lived on this land, poor Palestinians have had a daily diet consisting of whole wheat flat bread dipped in olive oil. The Prophet Muhammad ﷺ

reminded us to "Anoint yourselves with olive oil because it comes from a blessed tree." In *surah al-mu'minun, ayah 20*, Allah speaks of " a tree issuing from Mount Sinai which bears oil and seasoning for all to eat."

We don't need modern doctors to tell us about the obvious health benefits of eating olive oil and about how it has no cholesterol and improves blood circulation. We villagers have a hundred effective traditional remedies made from the fruit of the *sajarah al-mubarakah*, the blessed olive tree!

5. Ancient Finds

Palestine is an ancient land. Today, everyone in my country is affected by the ongoing conflict between the occupying forces and the Palestinian people. In the past, however, Muslim Palestinians, like their Muslim brothers and sisters of Al-Andalus, lived in peace with their Christian and Jewish neighbours. Our religion, *din al-haq al-islam*, is a religion of peace and tolerance and *al-Hamdulillah*, we have proved this many times throughout our history. To this day, some Palestinians still practise the Christian faith and live alongside Muslims in our villages and towns. The present conflict began more than one hundred years ago with the arrival of the first Zionists (fundamental Jewish nationalists) from abroad.

My people, the Palestinian Arabs, are descendents of the Canaanites, the earliest known inhabitants of Palestine. We did not arrive on the doorstep of Palestine as a people looking for a homeland. When Islam became the predominant religion in the Middle East, within a

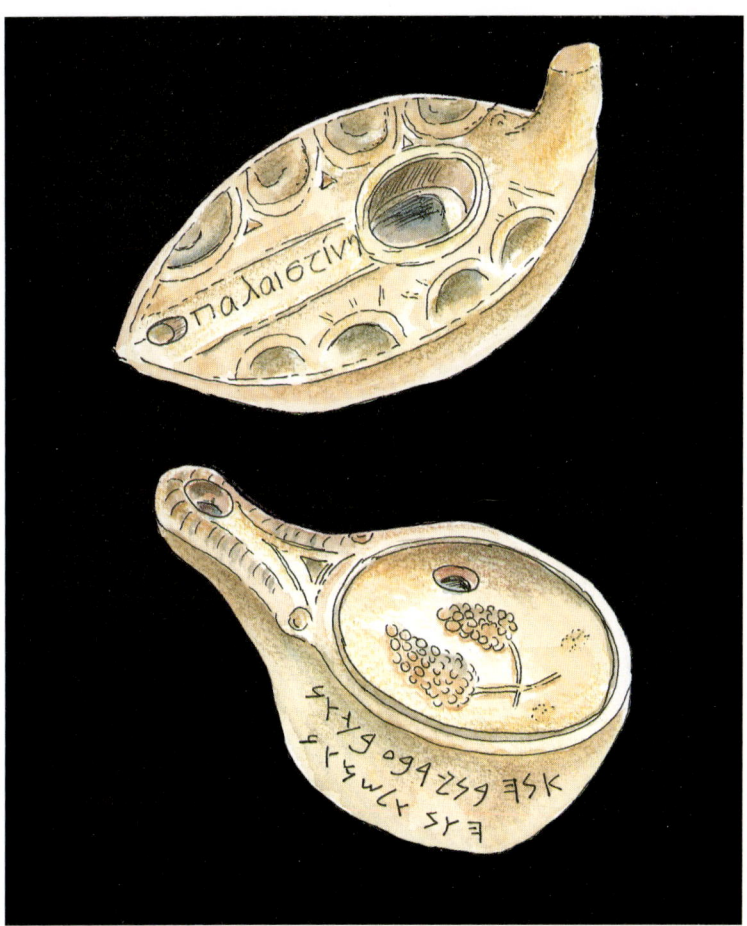

hundred years of the death of the Prophet Muhammad ﷺ, we too, the inhabitants of Palestine, became Muslim, *al-Hamdulillah*.

In many caves that dot the barren mountains near Bayt Zaytun along the edges of the Dead Sea, important ancient manuscripts (hand-written texts) have been found. In 1947, for example, a Bedouin shepherd from a village near Jericho discovered many parchment manuscripts rolled up as scrolls. Experts have examined these manuscripts and say these are the oldest existing

This is the beautifully carved wooden mimbar originally built for al-masjid al-aqsa by Nur al-Din al-Zenji, the ruler of Halab (Aleppo). He died before Jerusalem (al-quds) was liberated from the Christian Crusaders. In 1087 CE, however, Salah al-Din al-Ayyubi transported this mimbar to Jerusalem and placed it to the right of the newly purified mihrab of al-aqsa. This exceptional work of Islamic• art, having survived for almost a thousand years, was shamefully destroyed in a deliberate arson attack on al-masjid al-aqsa in August 1969. Some of the burnt remains of this historical mimbar can be seen today in the Al-Aqsa Museum next to the mosque.

examples of the Christian bible (*injil).

The extremely dry climate in our part of Palestine helps to preserve written records like manuscripts and fragile clay olive oil lamps (see illustration). We often find such lamps in the caves surrounding Bayt Zaytun. Inscribed on the top lamp is the Greek word *palaistini* ("Palestine'). On the second lamp is an Aramaic inscription. Aramaic is one of the oldest languages still spoken today. It is the only Semitic language still in use after 3,000 years! The Aramaic alphabet is derived from the Phoenician one that in turn gave us the Greek and Latin alphabets. The Aramaic alphabet, however, is the ancestor of our Arabic one.

According to Christian tradition, the Prophet 'Isa (Jesus) عليه السلام lived in our part of Palestine. Allah mentions in the Qur'an the miraculous ability the infant 'Isa عليه السلام had to speak at birth:

And [I came] confirming that which was before me of the Torah, and to make lawful some of that which was forbidden unto you. I come unto you with a sign from your Lord; so keep your duty to Allah and obey me. Lo! Allah is my Lord and your Lord, so worship Him. That is a straight path. (*surah al –'imran*, ayah 50)

As Muslims, we do not know precisely what language Prophet 'Isa عليه السلام might have spoken. It is possible, however, as Christians believe, that he spoke Aramaic and Hebrew, the two local languages at the time.

Insha'Allah, by everyone knowing our true history and respecting this ancient land called *filastin*, our people will once again be able to live in peace with all.

6. Palestinian Nomads

We Palestinians are attached to the soil of our beloved *filastin* like no other people. The Palestinians who truly know their homeland the best are the Bedouin or desert nomads. These people have traversed this land for thousands of years, moving from one region to the next in search of food and water for their goats, sheep and camels. It is very possible that some 4,000 years ago the Prophet Ibrahim عليه السلام came to Palestine (from the area of today's southern Turkey) guided by Bedouin nomads.

Unfortunately, it is becoming harder and harder for

the Bedouin to lead their nomadic way of life. Here in Palestine, the occupiers of our land are forcing the free roaming nomads into permanent settlements. The traditional life of the Bedouin, the real "men of the desert", is, therefore, slowly becoming a thing of the past.

Last year, in early spring, I saw a small tribe of Bedouin who had temporarily encamped outside our

village, just off the road leading to Jericho. This was an opportunity for me and many of my village friends to meet Bedouin children our own age. *Al-Hamdulillah*, my father took us to the Bedouin camp where we were welcomed by the *shaikh*, or tribal chief, in his *bayt sha'ar*, or black goat-hair tent.

These hand-made goat-hair tents are extremely practical shelters. Bedouin women are excellent weavers. To make a tent, they first take the rough, dark hair of their goats and spin it into yarn. This is then woven on ground looms (like the one in the illustration) into long bands of black hair fabric. Panels of this material are assembled to form the very light, yet durable "houses of hair". The tents permit even the slightest breeze to pass through them. If it ever rains, the moisture will cause the goat-hair threads to expand, thus making the tent waterproof.

The Bedouin tent is usually divided into three sections: a guest area on the left, a family area in the middle, and a kitchen on the right. Goat-hair tent dividers are also woven by the Bedouin women. *Masha'Allah*, because the desert nomads are always on the move, their possessions—mainly carpets, blankets and kitchen items—are few. But a visitor is an honoured guest and we were thus offered small cups of coffee made from freshly roasted and crushed coffee beans.

The Bedouin of Palestine—like all Palestinians, descendents of Ismail ﷺ—are deeply religious, *al-Hamdulillah*. As they do not live in villages or towns, their *masjid* is the open air! A very simply constructed *musallah* is made with a low semi-circular wall of rocks that forms a *mihrab* indicating the direction of Holy Makkah (see illustration).

Before we left for home, we prayed *salah al-maghreb* with the Bedouin. Our *imam* who led the prayer was the tribal leader. He recited in the most beautiful *tajwid* *ayah*s from *surah al-'imran:*

Without doubt, the people who have the best claim to Ibrahim are surely those who follow him—as does this Prophet and all who believe [in him] and Allah is the Protector of those who have faith.

7. The Traditional Market

The illegal occupation of our land in 1948 has changed Palestinian society forever. In the past, villagers like my father could easily transport their harvests of olives to nearby markets in Jericho, Jerusalem (*al-quds*) and Ramallah. Today, because of frequent checkpoints and roadblocks, it is sometimes very difficult to ship our olives, fruits and vegetables to the towns and cities of Palestine. Even in Bayt Zaytun, some villagers have reverted to bartering when they can not get their produce to market. Last year, for example, it was almost impossible to travel anywhere outside of our area near the Dead Sea. When my uncle could not sell his olive harvest in local towns, he traded his olives for meat, eggs and other necessities.

The Arab *souq*, or traditional market, is a basic part of our Islamic way of life. On special days of the week or month, lively, outdoor markets offer a wide range of goods for sale. Until very recently, I used to go with my father to the old covered marketplace in Jericho. It is called the *khan al-tujjar*, or "traders' market" (see illustration). Villagers from all around would come here to sell their fresh vegetables, fruits, garden-grown herbs and delicious Palestinian sesame seed "ring bread". Visiting the *souq* was also an opportunity to meet and chat with old friends from neighbouring villages.

For centuries, Palestinian women have sewn

beautiful traditional costumes whose designs varied from region to region. My mother, at the age of six or seven, learned from her grandmother how to embroider delicate patterns using a needle and thread. *Al-Hamdulillah*, these traditional dresses (*thawb*s) have become a symbol of pride in our rich Islamic cultural heritage. Such costumes are sold in the *souq* and are eagerly bought by Palestinians of all walks of life. *Al-Hamdulillah*, our cultural heritage is a rich one. Our occupiers, however, have a shameful habit of "stealing" our heritage and calling it their own. For example, even our traditional food, such as *falafel* (deep-fried chick-pea paste balls), they like to call their "national snack"!

The *khan al-tujjar* is an old trading centre that has served many generations of Palestinians under its roof. It has known good times and bad. *Insha'Allah*, this market like all others in Palestine, can once again be a bustling and thriving centre of local commerce.

8. My Village School

In Bayt Zaytun, we have a school, *al-Hamdulillah*. Here is the inside of my classroom. In the early morning, my younger brother and sis- ters have their classes here, but mine are in the afternoon. I usually sit in front of the teacher's desk, next to the globe. For me, the most exciting and interesting subjects are history and geography. *Insha' Allah*, I would like to be a history and geography teacher when I grow up and be able to write a history of my village.

As Muslims, we know the importance of education, *al-Hamdulillah*. The Prophet Muhammad ﷺ said, "The seeking of knowledge is obligatory for every Muslim." Each morning after the *fajr* prayers, I ask Allah for knowledge that will be of use to me. I remember the *du'a* of the Prophet ﷺ: "O Allah,

23

grant me benefit in what you have taught me; teach me what will benefit me and increase my knowledge ....” Allah also instructs us in the Holy Qur’an in *surah ta-ha, ayah* 114: “Say: ‘O my Lord [my Sustainer]! Cause me to grow in knowledge.’”

The occupation of Palestine has caused problems

for some pupils in neighbouring villages that do not have schools. These pupils, therefore, must study with us here in Bayt Zaytun, but the many checkpoints, roadblocks and curfews can sometimes prevent them from getting to classes. Last week, even our Arabic teacher could not reach school. On that day, we all stayed in our classroom and reviewed our lessons. Every Palestinian boy and girl knows that education is a great blessing from Allah. We understand that as pupils in school, our Islamic duty is always to seek knowledge and the pleasure of Allah.

Palestinian children are very good pupils, *masha'Allah*. We love to learn and are not afraid to study foreign languages. For example, in today's history class, as you can see, the subject of the lesson has been written in both Arabic and English on the blackboard. Our teacher first introduces the new lesson in Arabic. He repeats the highlights of it in English and finally allows us to summarize the lesson in English. He encourages us to speak English even if we make mistakes. *Masha'Allah*, this is very good advice!

Al-Hamdulillah, in all of Creation, Allah has blessed only we human beings with the gift of speech. The Prophet ﷺ said that knowing a second language is like being a second person with a second voice. Every time I speak or write English, I give thanks to Allah. We Palestinians have an important story that we want to tell the world. *Insha'*

Allah, when I am older, I will be able to tell this important story in English, my "second voice".

9. A Visit to Al-Aqsa Mosque

In the heart of Palestine lies the third holiest shrine in Islam, namely *al-masjid al-aqsa* ("the farthest mosque") in the city the Qur'an calls *al-quds* (Jerusalem). Last year, I made *ziyarah* here with my family. We left our village after *fajr* prayer and arrived in time for *dhuhr* prayer at *al-masjid al-aqsa* on the Temple Mount, the only place on Earth where all the Prophets of Allah (*'aleyhum al-salaam*) performed prayer in congregation. The Prophet Muhammad ﷺ was once asked by a woman: " ' O, Rasul Allah! Give us a ruling as to Jerusalem (*al-quds*).' And he said, ' It is the land of Resurrection and the Judgement assembly; go there and pray. For indeed, a prayer there is worth a thousand elsewhere.' "

The history of Jerusalem, a city holy to Jews, Christians and Muslims. is both long and complex. Throughout its history, it has experienced the repeated destruction and slaughter of its population. On two occasions, however, it witnessed outstanding examples of tolerance shown towards the inhabitants of the city. Firstly, in 638 CE, the Caliph 'Umar (*radhi Allah-u 'anhu*) personally accepted the surrender of Jerusalem to his Muslim forces. "Umar (*radhi Allah-u 'anhu*) entered the city on foot and no blood was shed; the property and places of worship of the inhabitants were all protected.

The construction of the beautiful mosque of *al-aqsa*, as we know it today, (see illustration) was first begun during the reign of the Umayyad Caliph al-Walid ibn 'Abd al-Malik ibn Marwan in 705 CE. By that

26

The distinctive colours of the Palestinian flag have a significant historical meaning. They are also found on the national flags of several countries of the Arab world: Syria, Jordan, Kuwait, Iraq, the United Arab Emirates and Sudan. The red triangle on the Palestinian flag recalls the red banner carried by Arab tribes during the early conquest of North Africa and Al-Andalus . For hundreds of years, the red flag was also the symbol of Islamic Spain. The black band represents the pre-Islamic sign of revenge and the colour of mourning adopted by the 'Abbasid Dynasty. The first Islamic dynasty, the Umayyads, chose white as a symbol of mourning and also in remembrance of the Prophet's ﷺ first battle at Badr. Lastly, the green band symbolizes the Fatimid Dynasty of Egypt and the colour of the blanket placed over 'Ali (radhi Allah-u 'anhu) who attempted to fool would-be assassins of the Prophet ﷺ. Since 1948, this flag has symbolized the hopes and dreams of countless millions of Palestinians and their brethren-in-faith world-wide.

time, the majority of Palestinians had become Muslim, *al-Hamdulillah*. The darkest days befell the mosque in 1099 CE when Jerusalem and its people were occupied by Crusaders from Europe who made the streets run with the blood of Muslims. For almost a century, *al-masjid al-aqsa* remained in the hands of non-Muslims who showed great disrespect by desecrating the *mihrab* (prayer-niche) and converting the building into military barracks.

The liberation of Jerusalem had always been the goal of Salah al-Din and his predecessor, Nur al-Din al-Zenji. It was, therefore, a triumphant moment when Salah al-Din finally entered the city as its liberator on Friday, October 2, 1187 CE, the holy *laylah al-mi'raj* (Night of Ascension). Before the city's liberation, Salah al-Din had said: "If Allah blesses us by enabling us to drive His enemies out of Jerusalem, how fortunate and happy we would be! For Jerusalem has been controlled by the enemy for ninety-one [*hijrah*] years, during which time Allah has received nothing from us here in the way of adoration."

With the return of *al-masjid al-aqsa* to Muslim control. we witness the second great example of tolerance shown on behalf of Muslims towards non-Muslims. During the peaceful takeover of *al-quds*, Salah al-Din forbade the ill-treatment of anyone, saying that such behaviour was unbecoming of a Muslim. *Masha' Allah*, Salah al-Din's generosity, sincerity, honesty and decency are all remembered even today not only by Muslims but by many nations whose once opposed him.

In one short week, Salah al-Din and his followers transformed *al-masjid al-aqsa* and the *al-qubbah al-sakhra* (Dome of the Rock) back to their original character. All parts of *al-bayt al-maqdas* (the Temple Mount) were purified with huge quantities of rose water and of course the first area to be cleansed was the *mihrab* of *al-masjid al-aqsa*. An exquisite carved wooden *mimbar* (pulpit) was transported from Halab (Aleppo) in Syria to be placed in al-masjid al-aqsa. With *al-bayt al-maqdas* all cleaned of debris, the first *salah al-jum'ah* in almost one hundred years was prayed on Friday, October 9, 1187 CE. The *khutbah* (sermon) delivered that day captured its great historical importance. "Jerusalem is the residence of your father Ibrahim , the place of ascension of your Prophet , the burial ground of Messengers and the place of descent of revelations....Glory to Allah who has bestowed this victory upon Islam and who has returned the city to

the fold of Islam after a century of perdition. Honour to His army which He has chosen to complete the conquest! And may salvation be upon you, Salah al-Din, son of 'Ayyub; you have restored the spurned dignity of this nation." Salah al-Din's victory was justifiably compared to that of 'Umar's (*radhi Allah-u 'anhu*) years before.

The spirit of Salah al-Din lives on in Jerusalem. Attempts have been made by the enemies of Islam to reoccupy the Temple Mount. For example, in August 1969, the beautiful *mimbar* of *al-masjid al-aqsa* was intentionally burned along with 1,500 square metres of the mosque. (The charred remains of this *mimbar* can be seen in the Al-Aqsa Museum). The great importance of *al-masjid al-aqsa* to all Muslims is made clear in the the Holy Qur'an in *surah al-isra', ayah* 1 :

Limitless in His glory is He who transported His servant by night from *al-masjid al-haram* [at Makkah] to *al-majid al-aqsa* [in Jerusalem] – the environs of which We had blessed—so that We might show him some of our symbols: for, verily, He alone is the All-Hearing, All-Seeing.

10. 'Eid in Jerusalem

Al-Hamdulillah, my family and I were able to be in Jerusalem to pray *salah al-'eid al-'adha* (the "holiday of the Sacrifice") last year. We had to pray outside on the well-worn marble pavement of the Holy Mount with some other 200,000 Muslims! We were facing *al-masjid al-aqsa* and behind us was *al-qubbah al-sakhra*, the beautiful Dome of the Rock. In our village mosque in Bayt Zaytun we are only a small *jama'at* . Can you imagine the feeling of reciting the *takbir* with so many people? *Allah-u akbar, Allah-u akbar, Allah-u akbar. La-illaha illah-u, Allah-u akbar, Allah-u akbar wa illa il-hamd.* Like us, many Palestinian families from all over the country try to visit Jerusalem in order to perform the *'eid* prayers and celebrate the holiday in this blessed city.

The octagonal (eight-sided) Dome of the Rock (see illustration) is the oldest Islamic structure that has survived from the earliest days of Islam. Allah in His Wisdom chose to transport the Prophet Muhammad ﷺ from Makkah to Jerusalem and from there to the Heavens. The Dome of the Rock, therefore, was built by the Umayyad Caliph 'Abd al-Malik ibn Marwan in 691 CE to preserve the site of this miraculous event. The Dome of the Rock lies at the centre of the Temple Mount and beneath its gold-covered dome is found the large slab of rock from which the Prophet Muhammad ﷺ ascended to the heavens on the steed *buraq.*

After *'eid* prayers were over, the *imam* offered a *du'a* asking Allah to make Muslims the eternal protectors of Jerusalem, the city sacred to the Prophets Ibrahim ﷿, Da'ud ﷿, Sulaiman ﷿, 'Isa ﷿ and Muhammad ﷺ. With our palms still raised in supplication, I personally asked Allah to bring peace to my beloved homeland – justice and dignity to all Muslims living under occupation. May my Muslim brothers and sisters from all corners of *al-dar al-islam* once again be free to worship with us here in *al-bayt al-maqdas. Amin.*

GLOSSARY

'Abd al-Malik ibn Marwan: The fifth Umayyad caliph

Badr: A outside city Madinah

Batil: Arabic for "false" or "erroneous"

bayt al-sha'ar: The traditional, portable black goat-hair tent of the desert Arab nomads

bedouin: Arab nomads of the Middle East

buraq: The horse-like animal brought to the Prophet ﷺ for his Night Journey to the Seven Heavens

al-dar al-islam: The "abode of peace"; all the countries that make up the Islamic world

du'a: An individual prayer made by a Muslim

falafel: Deep-fried chick pea paste balls; a tasty Palestinian snack food

fattoush: A healthful Palestinian green salad with toasted bread pieces

Fatimids: A Shi'ite dynasty (909-1171 CE) that ruled North Africa from Cairo

haqq: Arabic for "truth"; al-haqq, "the Truth", one of Allah's Beautiful Names

hijrah: The "migration" of the Prophet from Makkah to Yathrib (later Madinah) in September 622 CE; this event heralded the first year of the Islamic calendar

kafiyyah: The traditional Palestinian black (red) and white embroidered cloth head-dress worn by men

khan al-tujjar: "Traders' market"; an old traditional covered bazaar

khutbah: The Friday sermon delivered by an imam from the mimbar or pulpit of a mosque

laban: A thick, refreshing buttermilk drink

layleh al-mi'raj: The Night of Ascension of the Prophet ﷺ

majlis: The "sitting room" of a traditional Arab home

al-masjid al-aqsa': The mosque in Jerusalem; the third holiest site in Islam

maqloobah: A famous Palestinian dish made of rice, meat and vegetables

mihrab: The prayer niche in a mosque which indicates direction of Kabah

mimbar: The pulpit from which an imam gives the Friday sermon (khutbah)

Mount Sinai: A mountain in the centre of the Sinai Peninsula between Palestine and Egypt

musallah: A simple place for offering the ritual prayer

Nur al-Din al-Zenji: Ruler of Halab and Mosul who valiantly defended Muslim lands against the Crusaders

al-qubbah al-sakhra: The Dome of the Rock in Jerusalem

al-quds: The holy city of Jerusalem, the eternal capital of Palestine

Ramallah: An ancient Palestinian town close to Jerusalem on the West Bank

shajarah al-mubarakah: "The blessed tree" mentioned in the Qur'an; the olive tree

sini: A large, round metal tray from which food is eaten

souq: A traditional Arab open-air market

tajwid: The science which clearly explains the correct pronunciation and recitation of every letter and syllable of the Holy Qur'an

takbir: The exclamation "Allah-u akbar" (Allah is the Greatest)

thawbs: The beautifully embroidered traditional Palestinian women's dresses

'Umar: The second of the Rightly Guided Caliphs

al-Walid: Umayyad Caliph credited with the first construction of the Masjid al-Aqsa'

yawm al-hesab: "The day of accounts" the final day when all men's deeds are judged by Allah

zaaar: A delicious herbal seasoning made from dried thyme, toasted sesame seeds and marjoram

ziyarah: A visit or pilgrimage to Kabah or the Prophet's ﷺ Mosque or the Al-Aqsa' Mosque